Animals in Danger:
Orangutans

Written by Kerrie Shanahan

Flying Start
to Literacy®

T0363512

Contents

Introduction

Many animals around the world are in danger of becoming extinct. The World Wildlife Fund (WWF) currently has 50 animal species listed as endangered or critically endangered. All four of the great apes – gorillas, chimpanzees, bonobos and orangutans – are on this list.

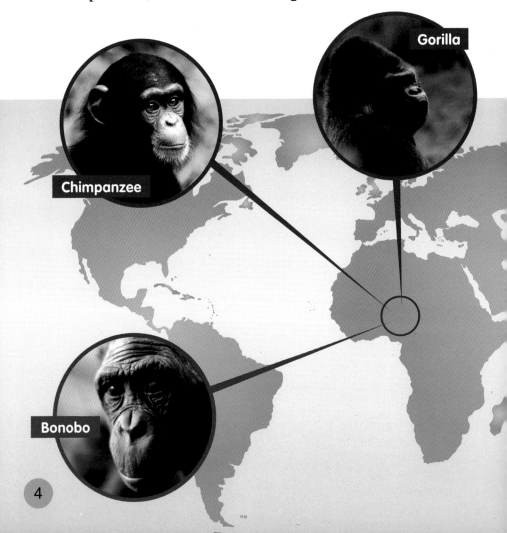

Gorilla

Chimpanzee

Bonobo

The great apes are endangered because of the loss of their habitat for mining, farming and logging. They are also endangered because of the illegal wildlife trade, disease and poaching. Their numbers are low and there is a high chance they could vanish from this planet forever.

Endangered
There is a high risk of extinction in the wild.

Critically endangered
There is an extremely high risk of extinction in the wild.

Orangutan

Orangutans are the only great apes that live in Asia.

There are two orangutan species:
- The Sumatran orangutan is critically endangered.
- The Bornean orangutan is endangered.

Of all the great apes, the orangutan is especially endangered because it is losing its habitat – the rainforest – on a grand scale. Large areas of rainforest are being cleared at an alarmingly quick rate. Without its rainforest home, the orangutan cannot survive.

But this is not the only reason why the numbers of orangutans are decreasing. Like all great apes, they are also threatened by hunting and the illegal pet trade.

Some people are working hard to save the orangutan from extinction. These people have established sanctuaries for injured and orphaned orangutans. They have also organised relocation programs for orangutans that have lost their homes.

But will these programs be enough to protect the orangutan? Can this vulnerable species be saved or will it disappear forever?

The scientific name for the great ape family is Hominidae. In scientific classification systems, humans are also placed in this family.

1 What are orangutans?

Orangutans are mammals and, as such, they are warm-blooded, feed their young milk and have hair. They live in tropical rainforests and depend on these forests for their survival.

About orangutans

Orangutans have many characteristics and behaviours in common with humans. Because of these similarities, the Malay people called them "orangutan", which means "person of the forest".

Caring for young

Orangutans are very nurturing. They feed their young, protect them and develop a strong bond with them. Orangutans give birth once every eight years, and feed their young on milk for six years.

During the first year of life, a young orangutan and its mother have almost constant physical contact. The young males stay with their mother for up to eight years and the young females are with their mother until their teens.

Intelligence

Scientists have discovered that orangutans are intelligent. They can reason and think to solve problems. They are able to learn about the different foods in the forest and where to find them. They create shelters using leafy branches to protect themselves from heavy rain.

Orangutans have the ability to use tools. Sumatran orangutans use sticks to pry open fruit with hard shells. Some Bornean orangutans use leaves to wipe their faces, in much the same way we use a serviette.

Living in the rainforest

There are only two rainforests in the world, on the islands of Sumatra and Borneo, where orangutans still live in the wild.

Food

Orangutans spend almost all their lives, about 95 per cent, high in the canopy of the rainforest, rarely coming down to the forest floor. They are the largest arboreal animals in the world and spend over half of their daylight hours foraging for food. They eat the leaves, fruit and fungi that grow on trees, as well as insects.

Orangutans can be up to 30 metres off the ground in the treetops.

Nests

High in the rainforest canopy, orangutans make nests using branches and large leaves. Most nights they make a new nest, but occasionally they will sleep in a nest that they have previously built.

Home range

Orangutans live in an area within the forest known as their home range. They move constantly throughout this area looking for food. These home ranges are about three to six square kilometres in size and often overlap with the home ranges of other orangutans. Usually, orangutans are not aggressive if other orangutans are in their home range.

Unlike the other great apes, orangutans are mainly solitary animals. Males live most of their lives alone and females live with their offspring until they are independent. If, however, a female orangutan comes across another orangutan, they may spend a short amount of time together, for example, if they are both feeding on fruit from the same tree.

Gardeners of the forest

Orangutans help to keep the rainforests where they live healthy. Because of this, they are sometimes called "gardeners of the forest".

Seed dispersal

Orangutans play an important role in keeping the rainforest healthy by spreading seeds throughout the forest. This is called seed dispersal. Orangutans mainly eat fruit. The seeds from the fruit move through the orangutan's body and are passed out as waste.

As the orangutan moves through the rainforest, the seeds are deposited and new plants begin to grow in different parts of the rainforest. Orangutans are the only animals in the rainforest that disperse certain types of seeds and therefore orangutans play an essential role in the survival of these particular plants.

Orangutans eat fruit. The seeds from the fruit are passed out as waste.

The seeds fall on the rainforest floor.

Soon, new plants grow from the seeds.

Letting in the sunshine

Plants on the forest floor need sunshine to grow. Orangutans open up the rainforest canopy by eating and using leaves from the top layer of the thick rainforest. This enables sunlight to reach the forest floor so new plants can grow.

Orangutans help to keep the forest ecosystem healthy and this, in turn, helps the other animals that live in the rainforest, many of which are also endangered. Due to the vital role that orangutans play in maintaining a healthy forest, many other animals would be endangered if orangutans become extinct.

Fewer leaves in the canopy means that sunlight can reach the rainforest floor, allowing more plants to grow.

Orangutans create openings in the rainforest canopy as they eat leaves.

Chapter 2
Why are orangutans disappearing?

Orangutans are disappearing from our planet. One hundred years ago, scientists estimate that over 230,000 orangutans lived in Southeast Asia. Today, there are only about 60,000 orangutans left in the wild. This decline in the number of orangutans is mainly due to the large-scale deforestation of the rainforests where orangutans live. The hunting and capturing of orangutans has also contributed to the rapid drop in numbers.

Over half of the rainforests in Sumatra have been destroyed in the past 30 years.

Cutting down the rainforest

Deforestation is the biggest threat to orangutans. People are clearing the rainforests where orangutans live to build houses and roads. As the population increases, the need for more land also increases and this puts the orangutans at further risk.

People are also cutting down rainforests to use the rich resources found there. The trees are logged to make products such as furniture, paper and timber for the building industry. Other plants are used to create fibres and medicines.

Rainforests are also cut down to mine for minerals such as copper, gold, silver, coal and diamonds.

Clearing rainforests to farm the land

People are destroying rainforests where orangutans live to make way for farms. Rainforests are burned or bulldozed so people can use the land to grow crops or to graze their cattle. Large companies have destroyed massive areas of natural rainforest so they can access the land.

Palm oil crops

On the islands of Borneo and Sumatra, home to the orangutans, huge areas of tropical rainforest have been cleared to grow oil palm trees. These trees grow very well in the same climate where tropical rainforests grow.

Palm oil is a vegetable oil produced from the fruits of the oil palm tree. It is used in a wide variety of products, ranging from chocolate, margarine, biscuits and cereals to shampoos, lipsticks and detergents. It is estimated that almost half of the products on supermarket shelves contain palm oil.

By 2020, the amount of palm oil the world uses is expected to double.

The rate of deforestation in Borneo since 1985. By 2020, it is projected that nearly two-thirds of the rainforest will have been cleared.

Oil palm trees have become a popular crop to farm because they are easy to grow and they produce more oil from less land than any other type of vegetable oil. The oil palm farms also provide employment. These farms have become a vital part of the economy for the islands of Borneo and Sumatra.

But when people cut down the rainforests and clear the land to grow oil palm trees, many orangutans are killed. Without their rainforest home, orangutans have no shelter and no food, and are at risk of dying.

Captured

Wild animals around the world are captured and sold as pets. This practice is against the law and is a huge international problem. Orangutans, like all the great apes, are in high demand as pets and, as such, are severely affected by this illegal practice. Some people think that owning an orangutan is a status symbol that shows they are rich and powerful.

Although it is illegal, there are still people who hunt and capture orangutans and sell them for high prices as pets. Many orangutans suffer and die when they are being captured or during the transportation process.

For every one orangutan that survives being a pet, there are three to five other orangutans that die because people do not know how to care for them properly.

Baby orangutans are the most sought-after orangutans for the pet trade and the younger the baby is, the more money it can be sold for. Because of this, many mother orangutans are killed so their babies can be taken from them and sold.

Many people who keep orangutans as pets do not know how to look after these wild animals. As a result, pet orangutans often become very sick and die.

The illegal pet trade is brutally cruel. It results in the deaths of many orangutans.

Hunted

The illegal hunting of wild animals affects many vulnerable species, including orangutans.

Orangutans are hunted and killed in the wild for a number of reasons: for their meat, for souvenirs, to protect crops and to obtain body parts to make medicines.

In some parts of Borneo, the local people hunt and kill orangutans so they can eat their meat. This practice has been happening for thousands of years and is usually done on a small scale where animals are hunted for food as needed.

Some people kill orangutans and illegally sell their body parts, such as the orangutans' skulls, as souvenirs. The body parts are also used to make medicines, and these medicines can attract very high prices.

When orangutans lose their rainforest home, they often have difficulty finding enough food. Starving orangutans may become desperate and wander into villages and farms on the edge of the forest to eat the crops. The farmers cannot afford to have their crops eaten so some of them kill orangutans that come onto their land.

A survey of the Kalimantan region in Borneo estimates that between 750 and 1790 orangutans are killed each year, just in this area.

3 Saving orangutans

Many people are taking action to save the orangutans. They are also trying to save the rainforest where the orangutans live because it is a significant habitat that is home to countless unique plants and animals, many of which are found nowhere else in the world. By saving the orangutans and their home, many other valuable living things are also saved.

What is being done?

Laws

Many governments around the world have introduced laws that protect orangutans. There are laws against criminals that hunt, kill or capture orangutans. The enforcement of these laws helps to protect the lives of orangutans.

In both Sumatra and Borneo, parts of the rainforest are protected by law, meaning that it is illegal to harm the forest in any way. Many people believe that more areas of rainforest need to become national park land to be safe from deforestation.

Relocation programs

As the rainforests where orangutans live are shrinking and the amount of food available is decreasing, more and more orangutans are struggling to survive. People have set up relocation programs to try to save these desperate animals.

Trained workers locate the troubled orangutans and use tranquilliser guns to stun them. The orangutans are then safely transported to their new home, usually in a protected area of rainforest, where they will have a much greater chance of survival.

Orangutan sanctuaries

Orangutan sanctuaries operate in both Sumatra and Borneo. At these sanctuaries, trained workers care for ill, injured or orphaned orangutans.

Sepilok Orangutan Rehabilitation Centre

Sepilok Orangutan Rehabilitation Centre, on the island of Borneo, was established in 1964. It covers an area of 41 square kilometres. The aim of the centre is to rehabilitate orphaned orangutans and, eventually, release them back into the rainforest.

The centre cares for orphaned orangutans by giving them medical attention and feeding them. Younger orangutans learn essential survival skills from the older orangutans as part of a buddy system. These skills include how to climb and forage for food. When the orangutans are ready, they are released into the rainforest reserve nearby.

The centre presently has about 25 young babies living in the nurseries, as well as about 60 to 80 older orangutans living free in the reserve. The rehabilitation of each baby orangutan lasts for about seven years, making it a lengthy and costly process but, ultimately, a very rewarding one.

27

What can you do?

The possible extinction of orangutans is a complicated problem and difficult to solve. But there are many things that people are doing every day to help save orangutans.

Recycling products

When products are recycled, there is less need for new products. This helps to reduce the demand for products such as timber and paper that come from rainforests. Therefore, there is less need to cut down forests.

Buying sustainable palm oil products

These products are made using palm oil that is grown in a sustainable way. This means that it comes from farms that have been established without destroying new areas of rainforest.

Products that are made using sustainable palm oil have a special label.

As more people visit the rainforests of Borneo and Sumatra, they learn about the plight of the orangutans. This helps spread the word.

Spreading the word

People are informing others about the plight of the orangutans and discussing ways they can help.

Conclusion

Orangutans are special and unique animals that are closely related to humans. Due to their similarities with people, orangutans have been studied for hundreds of years and they continue to fascinate us.

Orangutans live in tropical rainforests in Borneo and Sumatra and they play an important role in the health of their rainforest home by spreading seeds and allowing sunlight in so new plants sprout and grow. Orangutans are therefore crucial to the survival of many other plants and animals that live in these rainforests.

Unfortunately, orangutans are dying because their habitat is being destroyed to make way for settlements and farms. Orangutans are hunted, sold illegally as pets and even shot because they are considered by some to be pests. Sadly, because of all of these activities, orangutans are in danger of becoming extinct. Scientists warn that if things do not change, all orangutans in the wild could be gone in as little as ten years' time.

Everyone can help to save the orangutan and their home. Everyone can make a difference.

Glossary

arboreal an animal that lives most of its life in trees is arboreal

canopy treetops in a rainforest make up the canopy

economy the system when people produce, buy, and sell goods and services

ecosystem all living things, such as plants and animals, and non-living things, such as rocks, soil, sunlight and water, in an environment

endangered an animal that is very rare and in danger of dying out

extinct an animal or plant species that no longer exists

illegal something that is not allowed by law

rehabilitate to restore something to a healthy, normal condition

sustainable to produce a product in such a way that it does not completely use up or destroy natural resources